POSTCARD VIEWS OF NORTH DEVON

Saunton to Ilfracombe to Lynmouth

Tom Bartlett

* * * * *

Dedicated to the memorable summer and drought of '84

* * * * *

© Tom Bartlett

BACK COVER
Berrynarbor. *(1908 G). A wonderful rural photo postcard of village children and villagers outside the "Tom's" household of 24 & 25, Haggington Hill in 1908. It is all the more incredible that I have been given the names of all those in the picture by the smallest little girl, Lorna Richards, standing in road on right. Note the roads at that time – just broken stones compacted down by steam-engined rollers.*

First published by Badger Books in 1987
This reprint by Tom Bartlett, June 1990
Typeset by Lens Typesetting, Bideford, North Devon.
Printed by Maslands Limited, Tiverton, Devon.

About the author Tom Bartlett

Tom Bartlett moved from Middlesex to North Devon some twenty three years ago and before that spent many happy holidays in the county. He lives with his family in a cottage, directly under the 15th century Church Tower of St. Peters, in Berrynarbor, a quaint old world village which won the "Best Kept Village" title in 1985 and lies twixt Combe Martin and Ilfracombe. An avid collector of old postcards he has built up a large collection of North Devon and Cornwall and probably the largest and most comprehensive collection of Berrynarbor. Together with research carried out with local people and at Ilfracombe's Museum and library, has been able to produce this, his first book "Postcard Views of North Devon" almost entirely from his own collection.

This first volume of almost 300 picture postcards illustrates an area of North Devon centred on Ilfracombe but stretching to Lynton and Lynmouth to the east and Saunton to the south and will no doubt bring back nostalgic memories to those "not so young citizens" who browse through this book, whilst giving the younger generation an insight into the past.

As a founder member and past chairman of the North Devon Postcard Club which meets monthly at Barnstaple he has always found time to discuss cards and local history with anyone with similar interests and is always on the lookout for further cards! and he takes this opportunity of thanking the many dealers and particularly friends for their help in this connection. Framed enlargements of the majority of the cards appearing in this and subsequent volumes may be obtained by contacting the author direct (Combe Martin 883408).

POSTCARD VIEWS OF NORTH DEVON

Postcard collecting really became popular about 1903/1904 and was at that time the same type of craze as in modern times has been the introduction of the Rubic Cube, Hula Hoop and Trivial Pursuits! In fact no household would be without its Postcard Album and in cases each individual member of a family would have their own collection and album. We have to remember that in 1904 there were no televisons, radio was very primitive and most rural homes had no electricity or gas. This was the era of home, and well–supported outside entertainments, and Church up to three times on Sunday! thus the collecting of postcards became popular and children were for ever telling their friends of their latest cards and swopping any duplicates received. Until 1903 all cards appeared with "Address this side only" without a centre line dividing the back and was why small messages were written on the front, under or beside the picture.

Code for Postcard enthusiasts:

p/m Post Mark Date **c** = about, approx.
BG = B.C.Gribble, High St. C/Martin
G = Garratt of Bristol
HB = Harvey Barton, Bristol
J = Judges Ltd. Hastings
JWS = J. Welch & Sons, Portsmouth
LL = Louis Levy, Paris
N = National Series
PPC = Picture/Pictorial Post Card
PL = Phillipse & Lees, Ilfracombe
RT = Raphael Tuck & Sons Ltd.
SB = Senior & Co. Bristol
W = W.H. Smith & Son, Ilf. etc.
WB = Woolstone Bros. "Milton Glazette"

B & D = B & D Kromo
D = E.T.W. Dennis & Sons
G&P = Gale & Polden Ltd. Wellington Series
I = Ivy Series, J.V. Hughes, Penarth
JEJ = Jay Em Jay Series, Jackson & Son Grimsby
K = R.L. Knight, Barnstaple & Bude
LW = Lilywhite Ltd.
P = Pictorial Stationery Co. Ltd. London
PG = P. Goss, 2 The Crescent, Mortehoe
RA = R.A.P. Co. Ltd. London EC4 "RA" Series
* = BPADR EX23 OBR
ST = Stengel & Co. London EC
Wo = Woodbury Series
V = J. Valentine/Valentines

B = Batten Photo, The Capstone, Ilfracombe
F = Francis Frith & Co. Ltd. Reigate
H = Hartmann
IC = Ingram Clark, Ilfracombe
JS = J. Salmon Ltd. Sevenoaks
KB = Knight Brothers/Collection
M = Montague Cooper Lynton, Taunton, Burnham etc.
PB = P. Buse, Combe Martin
Ph = Photochrom Co. Ltd., Tunbridge Wells
S = E.A. Sweetman & Sons Ltd., Tunbridge Wells
T = Twiss Brothers, The Arcade, Ilfracombe
Wy = Wyndham Series
VB = Vickery Bros., Ilfracombe

A Devonshire Lane. *(c1904 P). This is but one of seven similar cards of a lane near Cherry Bridge, Barbrook, near Lynton, produced by four different publishers.*

Glenthorne *Nr Lynton & Lynmouth. (p/m 1904 P). The large estate and house are just in Devon after County Gate, between Porlock and Lynmouth. The zig-zag drive down to the house is about three miles long and drops 1,000 feet! It was then owned by a Miss Halliday who often gave permission for visitors to pass through her private grounds. Described in Page's Exmoor as "a pretty Tudoresque mansion pitched upon a tiny plateau, the only level spot for miles. On every side dark woods climb the giant hills, watered occasionally by diminutive streams, which tumble down to the beach over mossy rocks half concealed by fern brakes."*

At the turn of the century most farmers would reap their corn and after being left in "stooks" to dry, it would be collected in and threshed to remove the grains of corn, which were then taken to the local miller for grinding into flour. The majority of mills in this part of North Devon were all driven by water and four examples of these can be seen here.

Berrynarbor Mill. *(*p/m 1904). This mill was situated where Mill Park House of the Mill Park Camp Site, Berrynarbor is now. John Jewell was the miller there between 1883 and 1906 and therefore the girl in the picture is probably Miss Jewell. The mill was taken over in 1906 by Mr & Mrs Ernest Smith.*

Hele Mill, near Ilfracombe. *(p/m 1905 P). Showing the miller, Luther Solway, with a full cwt. sack of freshly ground flour, together with other members of his family. This mill alone is still operational and well worth a visit.*

Lynbridge Mill, Lynmouth *(c 1904 P).*

Woolacombe, The Manor Mill. *(p/m 1904 P). Time for a chat – note the corn sack truck and that the water wheel is not working, the water by-passing the wheel! The buildings already appear to be in a ruinous condition.*

Arlington Court. Whilst originally the Manor of Arlington was owned by the Raleighs, both it and the adjoining Manor of Loxhore came into the Chichester family in 1384 when John Chichester married Thomasine, daughter and sole heiress of Sir John Raleigh. It remained in the ownership of the Chichester's right up to the death in 1949 of Miss Rosalie Caroline Chichester, who since 1881 had been sole heir of the estates, and bequeathed the house, its collections and the entire Estate, to the National Trust. To the credit of the National Trust they have not only maintained, but improved and added to the house and estate, and it has thousands of visitors each year.

Arlington Vicarage, formerly known as the Rectory, and then the Glebe House, was built some time after 1825 when the Rev J H J Chichester was Rector of both Arlington and Loxhore. It is a well-built house with double bowed bays and has a finely curved staircase hall.

Kentisbury Ford, Nr. Combe Martin. (c1930 J). The Methodist Chapel on the left was built around 1850 and has two Memorial tablets on either side of the front porch. Sadly they have been desecrated with all the names and wording having been recently completely etched out. Fortunately a little further up the road the village shop still epitomises all that is truly rural.

Alford Terrace, Lynton. *(p/m 1911). The Terrace is at the top of the card and the Crown Hotel at bottom left with the Chapel in the centre, the road being Sinai Hill which then continues very steeply up to the Lynton and Lynmouth Railway Station off Shamble Way.*

Bratton Fleming, *the School House. (p/m 1905). This postcard was published by Miss Warren of the Post Office, Bratton Fleming; I wonder if anyone knows who they are? The message on the back reads "have sent you a PC of the school, the three people standing outside were the teachers when this was taken".*

West Down, The Square. *This photo postcard by Vickery Brothers, Photographers of High Street, Ilfracombe, must have been taken before or after school from the large number of village children around! West Down Post Office is in the centre and the Crown Inn on the left.*

Lee. *Old Cottages (P). Now known as "The Old Maids Cottage," was also known as "Swiss Cottage" and probably the most photographed building in Lee over the past century.*

Hunters Inn. *(c1904 F). Note the horse drawn carriage and brake. It is as popular now as almost 100 years ago with regular daily trips from Ilfracombe to visit Hunters Inn and Heddon's Mouth.*

Blackmoor Gate, Hotel and Restaurant. (RA). *A delightful card showing a thriving "Broom's Restaurant"; note old car and advertisement for Whiteways "Cydrax". Sadly it was completely burnt down in the '60's with the tragic death of a young maid, and was never rebuilt. Almost opposite were the Blackmoor Station buildings for the narrow gauge "Lynton and Barnstaple Railway" which connected with Combe Martin and Ilfracombe with firstly a horse-drawn service. Then in 1903 the railway provided two Milnes-Daimler motor charabancs which were sold off soon after being prosecuted for exceeding the speed limit when driving at 8, yes eight, miles per hour!*

Parracombe, near Ilfracombe. (c1906 T). *The horse drawn carriage is probably one of Sam Colwill's with a party of holidaymakers from Ilfracombe and they have just sampled one of the Parracombe-brewed "Crucombe & Sons" ales provided by "The Fox & Goose Family and Commercial Hotel".*

Ilfracombe to Barnstaple, Half-Way House. *(p/m 1906 P). This is on the old road to Barnstaple via Muddiford, and as well as the horse and cart, note the two bicycles, one in use!*

Combe Martin. *(p/m 1906 P). Kings Arms now "The Pack of Cards" and said to have been built in the seventeenth century by a man who won a considerable amount of money at cards. With this in mind he had it built with 4 floors, each floor had 13 doors and originally there were 52 windows!*

The Fox Hunters' Inn *on the Ilfracombe to Barnstaple Road, West Down. (c1930 RA). Still a very popular place, there appear to be three or four separate petrol pumps just in front of the left side of the Inn, and note the old car parked outside.*

The Blue Ball Inn, Countisbury, Lynmouth. (* p/m 1910 M). *An old coaching inn where the horses would often be changed after their hard and long pull up Countisbury Hill, when the main road was considerably narrower than it is today. Note the Blue Ball sign with intricate coiled cut steel support on the corner of the Inn, also the true "Pillar Box" in the pillar supporting the sloped-roof outbuilding.*

Rockford Inn, Brendon. (* p/m 1911 M). *A popular spot on the East Lyn river about two miles beyond Watersmeet.*

11

Muddiford and New Inn Hotel. *(c1930 K). The wording on the Inn reads "C.W. MARSTON, BEER, WINES & SPIRITS" and the small, old van outside has advertising on its side which includes ILFRACOMBE. Note that in common with most hostelries at about this time there is a petrol pump on the forecourt. The small shop on the right has advertisement signs for the Western Morning News and Lyons Tea. The foreground has now been completely cleared to form a large car park for the Muddiford Inn.*

Shelley's Cottage, Lynmouth. *(c1930). This card, published by J A Peddar of Lynmouth Post Office, shows the cottage named after the famous poet who, it is said, wrote "Queen Mab" here. The Shelleys stayed for 9 weeks in the summer of 1812.*

Saunton Sands III. (* c1904 P). *Grown almost out of recognition into the three-star Saunton Sands Hotel.*

Croyde Post Office. (p/m 1906 P). *A beautiful card of the thatched Croyde Post Office with a group of village children and what looks like the Croyde Post-Mistress. The small shop is covered with signs for Lifebuoy and Sunlight Soaps, and the windows with signs for Fry's Chocolate whilst over the door the sign reads TELEGRAPH OFFICE.*

Lynton and Barnstaple Railway.*(c1907 F). This unusual shot of the railway could have been taken shortly before Chelfham Viaduct where the lane between Goodleigh and Chelfham passes steeply down under the line before joining the main road from Snapper to Loxhore. After the Southern Railway acquired the line in 1922/23 they installed a larger concrete underline bridge which still stands to–day. Here's hoping that I am correct or that someone will tell me its true location! Informed by Bill Pryor of Lynton Station that the location is infact "Crossing first bridge out of Lynton Station at Barbrook Woods."*

View near Blackmoor. *(c1904 P p/m 1910). The picture below was probably taken at a spot now covered by the South West Water Authority's Wistlandpound Reservoir, near Blackmoor Gate.*

Lynton and Barnstaple Railway. *(c1907 F p/m 1910). The raised cutting near Parracombe was known as the "Parracombe horseshoe embankment". The Lynton and Barnstaple Railway was conceived by a group of gentlemen led by the influential London publisher Sir George Newnes who lived in Hollerday House, the large mansion he had built overlooking Lynton. Lady Newnes cut the first sod at Lynton Station in 1895 and the narrow gauge railway was constructed by contractors "James Nuttall" of Manchester, who went bankrupt in the process! The Railway opened in May 1898, almost a year later than scheduled, and many of the horse-drawn coach services came to an abrupt end. The line started alongside the main line at Barnstaple Town Station, passing through Pilton, Snapper, Chelfham, Loxhore, Bratton Fleming, Blackmoor Gate, Parracombe, Woody Bay Station and Caffyns Halt before reaching Lynton Station. The railway runs through nearly twenty miles of most beautiful North Devon scenery and it was a great loss when it finally closed on the 29th September, 1935. Had it survived it would today have proved a premier tourist attraction.*

Chelfham Station and Viaduct. *(p/m 1905 P). The station consisted of waiting room and booking office with a small signal box cabin with corrugated iron roof. The actual viaduct spanning Stoke Rivers valley was the largest single engineering item on the line, a graceful structure of eight brick arches each 42 feet wide and rising 70 feet in height over the roadway. The signals at each end of the viaduct should be noted, and the very large house on the right is Chelfham House.*

The Foreland Lighthouse, Lynmouth. *(p/m 1918 I). Sited on Foreland Point, the northernmost spot in the whole of Devon which commands open views of the Bristol Channel to the east, north, west and south-west and includes extensive views of the Welsh coastline on a clear day. The sailing yacht with the large "C" was one of the Cardiff Pilot boats often seen in and around Ilfracombe Harbour.*

Bull Point Lighthouse. *(c1904 P). This Lighthouse is now automatic, including the fog horn! The Trinity House Flag is flying, and someone appears to be camping on the headland.*

Ilfracombe

Ilfracombe Coat of Arms. *(p/m 1906). As produced in the Heraldic Series. The Coat of Arms was adopted in 1894 when, under the Local Government Act, the local Board of Health became the Ilfracombe District Council.*

Ilfracombe Harbour *1790 from an old painting. (c 1904 T). Note the chapel of St Nicholas; also the Parish Church and how Wales has been painted as appearing much closer than in reality. This painting indicates very clearly that the importance of Ilfracombe derived from its being a port, as can be seen from the location of the buildings, apart from the main street via Fore Street and High Street to the Parish Church.*

Ilfracombe in 1774.

Ilfracombe now.

"Ilfracombe Then and Now". *(p/m 1904 P). The "Then" being 1774 and the "Now" being 1903!*

Ilfracombe – A strange fish caught Oct 6th, 1906. Batten Photo. What a beautiful card – not only depicting a small shark but also the local fishermen, two children and harbour workers on the Pier. Could the elaborate cast iron stand be part of the set of scales? The man in the centre is Mr Williams with Fred Rudd just behind him.

"Mixed Bathers" at Ilfracombe. (* p/m 1908 Phillipse Photo). These two elephants (below) were regular visitors to Ilfracombe at the time, also visiting other West Country resorts as part of a travelling family circus called "Gingsters".

19

Harbour and Town from Quayfields, Ilfracombe. *(c1912 JR Wheeler, Promenade, Ilf).*
This card is full of interest with many large sailing ships and a few steam- driven boats in the harbour, and a good insight of many of the buildings around it.

Ilfracombe Harbour. *(p/m 1906 V).*
From an oil painting by R Warren Vernon.

A Corner of the Harbour. *(c1906 RT).*
This postcard is one of many produced by Raphael Tuck & Sons under the "Oilette Ilfracombe" series and on the back of this card is printed: "Ilfracombe Harbour is situated at the eastern end of the town. It is overlooked on the north side by the Lantern Hill, which protects it from the north-easterly winds. On the top of the hill is the old Chapel of St Nicholas, now surmounted by a lantern, from which the hill takes its name.

Ilfracombe Harbour. *(p/m 1914 LL).* Large Sailing Vessels at anchor and the one in the foreground is probably a Polacca ketch from Appledore, Braunton or Bideford. A Polacca has a straight mast without joint and the ability to sail backwards, useful for going over the 'Bar' into the Taw & Torridge estuary or out to sea.

"Stranded", Ilfracombe Harbour. *(c1897 T B).* This photo was taken by Batten on the 2nd April, 1897 of the barque "Aberlemno" of Swansea, 750 tons Register when she was towed into Ilfracombe Harbour by the Ilfracombe Lifeboat with the assistance from a rowing boat from Combe Martin. At 3.40 am the Lifeboat had been called out and after a good deal of searching in the dark towards Combe Martin found the "Aberlemno" caught up on Egg Rocks near Watermouth and Broadsands Beach. John Birmingham was Captain and bound from Glasgow to Rio with 1400 tons of coal. He encountered the full force of a tremendous gale and was driven about the Atlantic for 20 days! He sought the Bristol Channel and proceeded to Penarth with all sails gone. Having had them repaired, he proceeded with a crew of 15 down the Bristol Channel when, off Combe Martin he was caught in a heavy snow squall and was driven onto Egg Rocks near Combe Martin. In Ilfracombe the barque was temporarily repaired and then towed to South Wales for full repairs. Captain Birmingham was a well respected inhabitant of Ilfracombe whose son and later grand son, Tom Birmingham, were for many years the Campbell Steamers' agents in Ilfracombe.

The Harbour, Ilfracombe. *(p/m 1908.) A beautiful setting of the harbour with the towering heights of Hillsborough as a backdrop.*

Ilfracombe Harbour. *(p/m 1910 G). Note the tug with black-topped white funnel and the three large sailing boats, also the sailors' Bethel, the last two-storey building on the right. The tug would have been acting as a Pilot boat collecting full rigged ships from off Lundy and towing them into the Welsh Ports and vice versa. Longboats or gigs were kept in every small port and they would be rowed out to take in tow any sailing vessel that wished to enter or leave harbour. The maximum sized cargo sailing boats that Ilfracombe Harbour could handle safely were between 200 and 250 tons.*

The Harbour, Ilfracombe. *(c1906 T)*. The Cliffe Hydro Hotel can be clearly seen here top centre with Hillsborough Terrace on the left, whilst to the right are Rupertswood, Portland Street and part of Montpelier Terrace. Note all the fishermen's cottages and worksheds on the far side of the harbour and "Irwin's Pier Hotel" in the foreground.

Ilfracombe. *(p/m 1914 PL)*. This unusual view shows not only the Harbour area of Ilfracombe but also Rupertswood Terrace, the central town area and the Torrs and Torrs Park.

Paddle Steamer "Cambria" *(1912 B). Turning in the outer harbour; note Larkstone Terrace.*

Paddle Steamer "Britannia", Ilfracombe Harbour. *(p/m 1908 PL). Note the huge paddles! Post marked 1908, the message addressed to Miss Lucy Creek states "Hold your head up straight"! I believe Lucy is the pretty, smiling, young lady with scarve and without hat and lived in Sheffield House, Combe Martin with relatives at the Montebello Hotel in Ilfracombe.*

Steamers and Haymakers, Ilfracombe. *(Vinces, Ilfracombe). What a change from to-day; here we see approximately ten persons involved in cutting and stacking the hay whereas to-day the job would be done by one man and machinery. The passengers would clamber from one boat to the other until reaching the pier or their boat.*

*PS.LORNA
Campbells
Edwards Robertson*

Photo taken c 1894

RAVENSWOOD
Castle

WESTWARD HO!
Campbells

BONNY DOONE
Edwards Robertson

2. *Ravenswood.*
3. *Westward – Ho!*
4. *Bonny Doone.*
5. *Lorna Doone (Edwards Robertson)*
Photograph taken c 1896

Ilfracombe Inner Harbour. *(p/m) 1906 V).* How busy both the harbours and pier appear to be here.

The Passenger Fleet at Anchor (c 1904 ST). Six Paddle Steamers all moored in the outer harbour. What a sight, and what an income for the many businesses in 'Combe! Paddle steamers were capable of each bringing up to 600 day visitors from Bristol 74 miles away, Barry 35 miles, Cardiff 46 miles, Mumbles 22 miles, Penarth 42 miles, Swansea 25 miles, Tenby 40 miles, Weston-super-Mare 46 miles, whilst locally Lundy was 21 miles, Clovelly 19 miles, Lynmouth 12 miles and Minehead 26 miles. It is said that in the 1890's up to 5,000 people passed through the turnstiles daily. The photo was taken from the view point between the Vicarage of St Philip & St James and the Tawstock Hotel, Larkstone Terrace.

Paddle Steamer in harbour with Larkstone & Chambercombe in background. Note the lime kiln beside Larkstone Beach. *(p/m 1911 T).*

P.S. BRIGHTON
Pocketts Bristol Channel Steam Packet Company. c 1905-1911

St Nicholas Chapel, Lantern Hill, Ilfracombe. *(p/m 1910 RAP). This dates right back in time and its use as a lighthouse is recorded as far back as 1522 and has seen all types of occupation since then; the last family to live there were the Daveys who used to hang washing out all over the hill to dry! Since the early '70's the Ilfracombe Rotary Club have completely renovated the inside and open it every season for visitors to see this ancient chapel which is well worth a visit.*

Raparee Bathing Cove, *Ilfracombe. (c1920 JS). This is from a water painting by AR Quinton who was born in Peckham, London in 1853 and was exclusively employed by JH Salmon, Postcard publishers, from 1911 when he was 58 until his death in December, 1934 aged 81. Of particular note is the bandstand on the pier.*

Rapparee Cove, Ilfracombe. *(* 1907 Phillipse). Things were different then! Note the ladies bathing huts, with those on the left able to be wheeled to the sea edge whilst those on the right with handles had to be carried.*

The Great Gale at Ilfracombe
(* 1910). This view shows clearly the enormous amount of damage to Ropery Meadow Gardens caused by the tidal wave. This is Card No 22 of about 30 photograhic cards produced.

The Great Gale at Ilfracombe on 16th December, 1910, or to be precise, a large tidal wave which breached the sea wall between "Preachers Rock" and the Ilfracombe Hotel, and caused damage to the entire area in front of the Pavilion and the terrace of shops and restaurants facing Ropery Meadow.

Coach and Four White Horses. (*1906) Sam Colwill, the man with the white beard, was the coach-operator and was once also town mayor. His son Tom Colwill is the driver, and the guard, also with top hat and brass buttons, was Bert Gear. They are all seen outside Colwill's Office next to the Queens Hotel.

This coach and four (* 1906) is posing for the photograph outside the Methodist Church, Wilder Road and has at least seventeen persons onboard!

Bridgeman's Car with seating for only five passengers plus the driver (c 1923 V).

A charabanc (c1912) outside the building opposite the now "Scarlet Pimpernel Garage" at the top of Portland Street; note the solid tyres and headlamp, also the upholstery, coach-building and double running board. However, if it rained or there were cold winds passengers were very open to the elements, hence all the overcoats and hats.

Blue Cars Pneumatic-tyred charabanc pictured outside the Cliff Hydro Hotel on the main road towards Hele Bay, Combe Martin. (Photo Post card by Grattan Phillipse, Ilfracombe).

Off for the Day. Six or seven charabancs, all with solid tyres, line up on the main road outside the Cliffe Hydro Hotel. The first two are Daimler cars whilst the fifth appears to be a Rolls Royce. It seems they used to line up at this spot just so that photographs could be taken.

The Instow Beagles and followers passing the United Reformed Church in Ilfracombe High Street on 22nd February, 1909. Note on the left the Fish Shop and Barbers pole with "SHAVING" sign hanging from it. (* 1909 PL).

R Martin the Ilfracombe Town Crier, outside Capstone Parade. (p/m 1907 W). He was alleged to be the only mounted Crier in England and there are postcards of him in Lee, Woolacombe and Combe Martin, so one wonders if, when he had something really to cry about, he travelled to all the local villages and towns?

Visit to Ilfracombe of EJ Soares, Esq in 1904, prospective Conservative Member of Parliament, to give an address. (1904 Phillipse, Ilfracombe).

Ilfracombe Camp Sports, *7th, August, 1910 (* 1910 B). Taken to the east of the Pavilion, this could have been the annual sports day held every summer for the children of Ilfracombe on Ropery Meadow.*

A beautiful card (c1904) showing children in **Bicclescombe Park by the Wishing Well.** It is amazing that all the children, boys and girls, are all wearing hats of different sizes and shapes!*

Interior of **Victoria Pavilion** *(c1906 P). Built like a giant "glass house" in Queen Victoria's reign at about the same time as the famed Crystal Palace, London, with glass set into the iron framework. Concerts were often held inside and visitors would congregate there whenever the weather was at all inclement.*

Church Parade, Ilfracombe. *(c1906 V). At the turn of the century residents and visitors alike would attend one of the many churches at least once on the Sunday, and some would attend up to three services. Best clothes were kept by all for wearing only on Sundays and it gave the ladies their opportunity to "parade" through the town. The hotel on the right is the Imperial Private Hotel and had magnificent wrought-iron balustrades and arches.*

Ilfracombe Hotel. *(c1906 B & D).* This is a beautiful card showing the Ilfracombe Hotel at its best, the small building on the left was the Hotel's laundry and is still standing, in use as the Ilfracombe Museum. It is filled to the brim with all sorts of historical and interesting items and is certainly worth a visit.

Promenade and Grounds looking west from Gilbert Hotel, Ilfracombe. *(* p/m 1930 Publisher RS Short, 40 High Street, Ilf).* This card, postmarked 1930, shows how cars were being used as taxis although the horse and carriage has not completely disappeared; see right foreground. The Union Jack flies over both the Ilfracombe Hotel and outside the Collingwood Hotel.

Runnacleave Hotel, *Ilfracombe. (p/m 1915 VC & Co).* This card shows the very grand entrance to the Runnacleave Hotel which extended from the pavement right up to the main doors; one can almost envisage a "Palm Court Orchestra" playing there.

Wilder Road. *(p/m 1928 V).* The Grosvenor, Berkeley & Osborne Hotels, and the entrance to the Runnacleave Hotel and amazingly no sign of any traffic at all! The sign on the left advertises Rapparee Beach, which could be reached by ferry boat and where "Mixed Bathing" took place!

Berkeley Hotel, Ilfracombe. *(c1930 Southwood Exeter).* This is very much an artist's impression and certainly appealing and majestic, even down to the then very modern car.

Ropery Meadow Gardens. *(p/m 1908 ST).* The memorial has long since disappeared, St Philip & St James Church, Gilbert Grove and the Collingwood Hotel surround the grass, incidentally called Ropery Meadow due to the fact that there was at one time a thriving business for making heavy and thick hemp ropes for shipping.

The Band Stand & Capstone Parade.
(p/m 1919 HB).
Taken about 1919, before the construction of the "new front"; note pram and boy with wooden pair of stilts. What a shame that Ilfracombe Council agreed for the Band Stand, erected in 1894, to be dismantled and sold in the 1960's.

"The New Front" Ilfracombe. *(p/m 1924 Phillipse).* A very changed Ropery Meadow taken in 1924; no memorial, completely walled and pillars with lanterns on top. The gardener rolls the bowling green of the east half, whilst the other half has been turned into a putting green.

Ilfracombe from Capstone Hill. *(p/m 1909 T)*. Horse drawn carriages wait for customers. The view shows Montpelier Terrace top centre, and both Rupertswood and Coronation Terrace on the left, and the road we are looking up is Mill Head leading to Fore Street. The houses top left are Castle Hill and Terrace, and Highfield Road.

Capstone, North Parade, Ilfracombe. *(p/m 1914 T)*. I would imagine that this was taken about 1906 and on a Sunday (Church Parade?). In those days the sun was considered injurious hence the wide use of umbrellas and parasols. This card found its way home from Western Australia!

The Beach, Wildersmouth. *(* c1906 Wo)*. Note the children, and a lady in a wheeled chair, all watching the Punch & Judy show on the beach. The ill-fated Arcade and Hotel are top centre left, at the top of Arcade Road, and were burnt down in 1984.

The Tunnels Bathing Beaches. *(c1899 F). This old and beautiful card shows how modest the Victorians were, using wheeled bathing huts to ensure no one could see them entering the sea. Even with a magnifying glass it is extremely difficult to find any skin showing at all. They would find things very different nowadays!*

The Tunnels Bathing Pool and Beach *ICB 26 (p/m 1929 LW). A much later card shows how busy the tunnels beaches often were. It is interesting to note that the Tunnels were opened to the public in 1836, together with "hot and cold Baths" in the large ornamental building to the left of the entrance. There were separate beaches for the Ladies and Gentlemen and a bugler was strategically placed high up on the rocks and would blow a warning blast should any of the men start walking or swimming towards the Ladies Beach!*

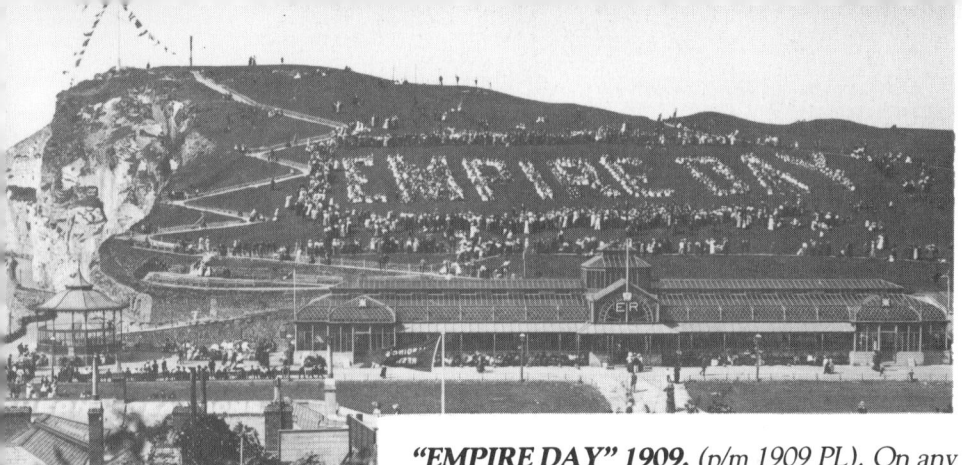

"EMPIRE DAY" 1909. *(p/m 1909 PL). On any great day it was customary for the children from the local schools to congregate on Capstone Hill behind the Victoria Pavilion and under direction form up into letters commemorating the particular event. On this card note E R and crown over the pavilion for King Edward VII. The custom has been re-established by the Ilfracombe Comprehensive School who in 1986 formed the word "LIVE AID" – alas no official postcard however!*

"GEORGE & MARY". *Coronation Day in 1911. (* p/m 1911 Coronation Souvenir). A day of strong easterly winds judging by the bunting and flags.*

"PEACE". *(* 1919). Commemorating the end of the First World War on July 19th, 1919. According to the back of the card Mr Wilf Robins of "Robins Garage" is at the top of the letter "C" whilst Mr Wilf Thorne, JP, is in the centre of the letter "P" and Mr Stan Hiscock is in the centre of the first "E".*

38

Ilfracombe's Voluntary Aid Detatchment taken on 24th January, 1919, showing the entire contingent with Dr Osborne left of centre.

The Ilfracombe RGA Volunteers Band heading a procession of the Foresters to their annual Church Parade Service on Sunday 11th February; a National Rally at Ilfracombe in 1906 when the Preacher was the Rev F G Walker.

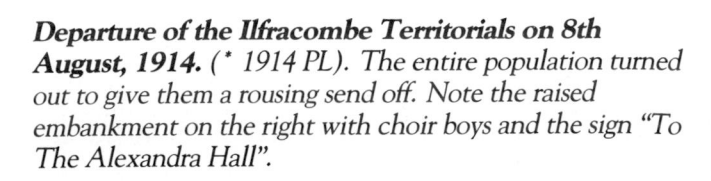

Departure of the Ilfracombe Territorials on 8th August, 1914. (* 1914 PL). The entire population turned out to give them a rousing send off. Note the raised embankment on the right with choir boys and the sign "To The Alexandra Hall".

High Street, Ilfracombe. *(p/m 1904 N). Two views of the High Street: the first is taken from outside the Clarence Hotel. The footpath and also part of the road was then raised from the Baptist Church, just after Oliver's Shoe Shop (still there) right up to where the road leads off Springfield Road.*

Ilfracombe High Street. *(p/m 1907 W). The lower card was taken from outside Thomas's, the Jewellers.*

Adelaide Terrace, Ilfracombe. *(c1904 B). Dozens of chimney pots, and the rear of Oxford Grove houses on the far left. This real photo postcard by Batten must be one of the first taken of the complete Terrace and shows how very much more impressive such a terrace is when all the houses adopt the same white external finish, particularly with the black-painted wrought ironwork balustrades over the pillared entrances.*

The Railway Hotel, High Street, Ilfracombe. *(p/m 1905). Situated to the right of where the Gateway Supermarket is now and the entrance to the rear remains to this day.*

Ilfracombe, Fore Street. *(p/m 1906 RT). From a painting by HB Wimbush. "Ilfracombe, once a seaport of some importance, is now a rapidly increasing watering-place, whose popularity is as well established as the reputation of its mild winters. Fore Street used to be its main street, but there are many new squares and terraces now, though none so picturesque as the steep old causeway shown here, running straight down to the harbour."*

St Philip & St James Church, Ilfracombe. *(p/m 1909 JWS). This church was built and brought into use about 1863, and has always had an evangelical spirit and particularly welcomes visitors to its services. Note "Price's Boarding House and Restaurant" on the left and The Cliff Hydro Hotel and part of Hillsborough Terrace, top right.*

St Peter's Church. *(p/m 1905 P). Situated in Highfield Road just opposite the top of Oxford Grove, the church has an elaborately carved pulpit.* ▶

Holy Trinity Parish Church, Ilfracombe. *(c1903 T) which has had a continual line of incumbents since Oliver de Tracy in 1263! The church has a magnificent wagon roof with finely carved decorative bosses which were lovingly restored in 1961 when Rev Arthur Chandler was vicar and who later became Rural Dean of Barnstaple.*

Tombstones in Parish Church.
(c1904 B).
Commemorating the nine Ilfracombe Centenarians who died between 1784 and 1897.

The Bowling Green, Ilfracombe. *(p/m 1905 H). This card must have been taken shortly after the club had been formed and is still flourishing to-day at its Highfield Road site.*

43

Ilfracombe from the Cairn. *(c1906 V). This shows a very busy Ilfracombe Station with a great number of trains and carriages around. Look for the signal box, signals and the engine sheds. The large houses on the Torrs can also be seen, with the Granville Hotel standing out against the skyline on the top right of picture.*

Cairn Top, Ilfracombe. *(p/m 1918 JWS). A train is just entering Ilfracombe Station on the far right. There appears to be a garden house where the "Round House" now stands.*

Slade and Cairn Top, *Ilfracombe. (c1908 T). The line of the railway and a signal can be clearly seen, as also the footpath, still there today, running behind the terrace of houses and then under the railway to continue its climb up the Cairn.*

Four View "Card of Ilfracombe". (c1904 P).
1) Torrs Walk and Cafe that was on the top; 2) The Parish Church; 3) Donkeys at Watermouth; 4) The Thatched Cottage at Chambercombe also known as Chambercombe Cottage, the Hermitage, and now The Thatched Inn).

Higher Slade, a Devonshire Lane. (p/m 1928 S). A really rural picture, and one that apart from the disappearance of trees, remains very much the same today.

Torrs Walk from Ilfracombe Station. (c1908 W). The large hoarding with the advertisements for Vinolia, Rogers Beer and Cyders has a sign Devon BPC above it – whatever the letters BPC might stand for? The road is the town end of Slade Road, where Broad Park Crescent is now.

Not only **Chambercombe, Ilfracombe.** (p/m 1908 EO & Co) but also **"Xmas Greetings"**!!

Chambercombe Farm, Ilfracombe. (c1906). (The Haunted Manor!) On the back of this card are printed the following words:
*"'Tis said the gentle Lady Grey,
Once stayed where Champernoune's held sway,
In this ancestral Hall;
And as she wandered through the glade,
Little thought she the cruel blade,
On her fair neck would fall."*

Hele Village. (c1908 T). An unusual view of Hele, showing the oldest part of the village and the lane running up and to the left is the old coach road to Berrynarbor.

Hele Bay. *(c1906 V). This card from about 1906 shows Lewis's Beach Cafe and the small Beach-side terrace of houses, with a rowing boat tied up to a monstrous sized buoy!*

Hele Valley. *(c1906 V). The top card shows Foxbeare Road and gasometer and gasworks in the foreground; Hillside Terrace and the terrace of houses bordering Watermouth Road.*

Watermouth Road, Hele Bay. *(c1906 RT). The lower card is interesting in so far as there are no buildings at all on the left until the gas works. Hele Hotel can be plainly seen on the right and the council houses of Hillside Terrace stand out below Hillsborough. These were pulled down some years back after a landslide left the council worried that they could be the next to take a "slide down the hillside"!*

"Sumwhere to Ilfracombe". (p/m 1913). *The message on the back says: "We are having such a lovely time here that this will be our state on returning."*

"No flies on the Beer at Ilfracombe", "Post from Ilfracombe". *both with 12 pull out views*

"There's No Flies on the Beer at Ilfracombe". *(p/m 1927 V). This mailing novelty postcard by Valentines was sent at the price of a letter if more than the name and address of sender was written. This particular card has been overstamped with "1d To Pay, Liable to Letter rate" all because Charlie wrote: "Having a lovely time came by Steamer from Cardiff".*

48

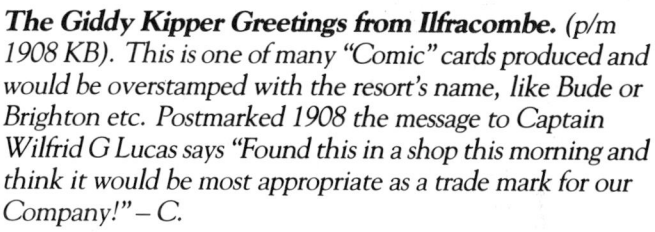

The Giddy Kipper Greetings from Ilfracombe. (p/m 1908 KB). This is one of many "Comic" cards produced and would be overstamped with the resort's name, like Bude or Brighton etc. Postmarked 1908 the message to Captain Wilfrid G Lucas says "Found this in a shop this morning and think it would be most appropriate as a trade mark for our Company!" – C.

The Last Train from Ilfracombe. (p/m 1910 V). This "comic" card was sent from Ilfracombe in 1910 and again was the type of card where the name of the town was inserted and so could be sold all over the country.

"The Smart Set Entertainers". *(p/m 1905 PPC). They gave concerts every year in Ilfracombe from about 1904. There is little doubt left as to which gentleman is the pianist!!! And perhaps a monocle was part of the act?*

Coastguard Houses *on road between Ilfracombe and Combe Martin. (p/m 1934) Built about 1930, these were fully occupied by Coastguard personnel right up to the late '70's, but apart from the house marked with a cross, were all sold off a few years ago.*

Coast Road to Watermouth. *(p/m 1914 T). An early card showing the road to Combe Martin, the Golf Course and very small club changing room. The strip of land that the road meanders around is fully cultivated with neat rows of vegetables, but this area has been subsequently infilled and the road now takes a direct line and then passes the coastguard houses which were built about 1930.*

Berrynarbor

Introduction

Berrynarbor was known as "Hurtesbury", (Domesday Survey in 1086), and later passed to the Nerbert family and became known as Berry Nerbert. The Church is first mentioned in a deed of 1133 when Nicholas de Plymptone is the first recorded rector in 1261. The Berry family appeared during the reign of Edward 1st (1272-1307), and their 'Elizabethan' Manor House was built c1480 and still stands west of the church. Undoubtedly, of all the people born in Berrynarbor, John Jewell (1522-71) must be the most renowned. Born at Bowden Farm, Sterrage Valley, he became Bishop of Salisbury and author of the famous 'Apologia pro Ecclesia Anglicana' of 1562 which Queen Elizabeth 1 ordered to be read in every church in her kingdom. It is not generally known that his greatest opponent, Thomas Harding (1516-72) who gave up protestantism and retired to Louvain, was born in the next parish of Combe Martin.

The Berry family retained the village until 1708 and in 1712 the greater part of the parish was purchased by J.D. Bassett Esq. in whose family it remained until the two large sales of 1921 and 1924. These sales by auction completely broke down the estate into individual properties but gave the freehold to many of the tenants, whilst others who could not afford to buy were turned out.

The small Independent Chapel was built c1830 and the larger and more modern section was added about 1887 and the National School was built in 1848 for 150 children and is still in use today with about 50 pupils and 2+ teachers.

It is interesting to note that the population for Berrynarbor (including Berry Down) in 1850 was 899 inhabitants and there were 27 farmers, 4 blacksmiths, 6 shoemakers, 3 shopkeepers, 6 carpenters, 3 tailors, 3 (Stone) masons, 3 beerhouses, 2 licenced victuallers (Globe & Unicorn) and 1 corn miller. By comparison in 1985 Berrynarbor was judged "BEST KEPT VILLAGE IN DEVON" and the population was c600 inhabitants with 20+ farmers, 1 blacksmith, 3 shopkeepers, several builders, several hotels and guest houses, 1 licenced victualler (Globe), several licenced restaurants, 8+ caravan/camping sites and, of course, Watermouth Castle with all its attractions for visitors. Berrynarbor has thus changed from a truly farming/agricultural parish into a farming/tourism dominated parish with an ever-increasing tendency towards tourism.

St Peter's Church has an impressive perpendicular tower of 96 feet in height and of four stages and very similar to St Peter's Church, Combe Martin and St Nectans at Stoke (Hartland). The Tower has clocks on two faces, and six bells.

Berrynarbor *No 137. (c1904 PL). This photographic postcard by Phillipse & Lees of Ilfracombe shows not only the church but also Haggington Hill and part of the Manor Hall.*

"Berrynarbor" *Garratt No 14. (c1904 G). A very early card of Berrynarbor village, church, chapel, manor house, Tower Cottage, Bessemer Thatch, and Haggington Hill with its cultivated strip gardens. Many of the village cottages were thatched and Betsy Leaworthy's cottage is just showing behind the Manor House, later to be hidden by the new Manor Hall. Several children and young ladies are playing outside the school in the road.*

Back of the card is page 4 of a message sent and reads "and peered into the window of the only other shop the place contains, where you see biscuits and ribbons and pencils and sweets all on the same counter. We wanted some sweets but the flies were so numerous. On the way home we went by the inland road, past all these white cottages" (Hagginton Hill). The shop referred to is undoubtedly the Dormer Cottage (House) shop run by Mr Klee.

"Bowden Farm, Berrynarbor" *This seemingly rare photo postcard of Bowden Farm reads on the back "John Jewell, Lord Bishop of Salisbury was born here in 1522, educated Barnstaple Grammar School and Merton College, Oxford; 1560 appointed Bishop.*

"Berrynarbor" *Garratt No 16. (c1904 G). The card shows Pitt Hill, Fuchsia Cottage, old Post Office and the knife-sharpening barrow pushed round from village to village by Jim Glass, who did not live in the village but travelled all over North Devon. He is mentioned in "Memories of Old Bradworthy" by Cecil T Collacott, as Johny Glass, who earned a few coppers as a scissors grinder and occasionally he would ask for a can of hot water and a cold potato, no doubt expecting much better. The first building on the left is where the Bassets of Watermouth Castle would stable their coach and horses whilst they went to church.*

The Village, Berrynarbor. *(c1922 JS).* From one of four watercolours by the artist H Hughes Richardson in 1922 for the postcard publishers J. Salmon of Sevenoaks, the card depicts the National School, blacksmiths shop and Church steps. The dwelling on the right became the new Post Office and is still such to date.

Capel Cottage. *(c1925 G).* This must be one of the most photographed cottages in Berrynarbor and has also been called "Wayside Cottage" (c1906) and "Rayburn Cottage" (c1920). About 1903/4 Mrs Snell lived here as a widow with her four children, Arthur, Nelly, Walter and Mabel, and did the washing for the Vicarage. Sir Reginald Beatty Wolsely and his wife Lady Marion Elizabeth Wolsely also lived here until he died on 9th July, 1933 aged 61 and she followed him less than a year later on 23rd June, 1934 aged 56 years. The roof showing is where Sam Harding, the village blacksmith, used to live.

"Berrynarbor" *(Garratt No 7. c1904 G). Jim Kemp just outside his cottage, No 46; his wife was the village mid-wife around 1911. The man with the push-bike is Jim Hancock, who lived at 51. The Village (Tower Cottage) with his wife, Meta, and had a daughter Emma Corney Hancock, and a son called Denzil who died when he was only six years old and is buried in the church yard. The house seems to have been in a poor state. Dormer Cottage (House) was then a shop kept by a Mr Klee of German extraction (it was said his father came over with the German band that played every season in Ilfracombe).*

"In Berrynarbor" *Garratt No 16. (c1904 G). One of Garratt's first photographs of the village and shows Sam Harding's blacksmith shop on the right as well as the school complete with bronze bell on the roof and a fuchsia hedge inside the iron railings. The man carrying a sack is probably Sam Harding, but the identity of the lady in long dress typical of Victorian times, is not known.*

"Berrynarbor Inn" *Garratt, No 108. (c1925 G). This lovely photo by Garratt of the Globe Inn epitomises the old village Inn. Note the word "BAR" over the right entrance, and the village petrol pump selling Shell Mex. It follows that landlords in the 20 and 30's not only pumped beer! Mr Will Bray was landlord until March, 1921, when the inn was included in the first Watermouth Estate sale. He also collected the rates and taxes for the castle and distributed the Parish Relief, about 5/- per week in 1900. Charlie Cornish was the next landlord and had a daughter Doris. In about 1923 he had the petrol pump installed on the front forecourt. Charlie Blackmore took over about 1930.*

"In Berrynarbor 22." *(c1904 G). Outside the thatched Brookside Cottage, 63 Silver Street, next to the cottage that is now the Post Office. Whilst I have never been able to name any of the children, the occupants of the cottage were Ben and Polly Draper with children Polly, Lucy and Evram and Mr C Huxtable lived in No 62 Silver Street, (now the Post Office).*

"In Berrynarbor" *Garratt No 57. (c1908 G). The two Street sisters, Tilley and Dawkis, outside their cottage, 71 Higher Sterridge Valley, feeding the chickens and ducks. Mr Evram Street and his wife had 5 or 6 children, Jack, Bill, Dick, Lizanne and Nelly. Also shown is Barn Cottage, No 69, where Will Blake lived around 1922 . He was a 'Stone-Cracker'. The small tap house (which supplied water to all the nearby cottages) still stands complete with tap but, alas, no roof.*

"Sterrage Valley, Berrynarbor" *Garratt No 61. (p/m 1904 G). The children could be members of the Street family. In 1923 Dan Jones lived in the first cottage and Mr and Mrs Loveday-Jones in the next cottage.*

"Berrynarbor 3, near Ilfracombe" *No V44 (p/m 1913 V). Another Valentine's real photo showing the whole village from a slightly different angle. Note the absence of houses or bungalows on Barton Lane or Birdswell Lane. Also note Moules Farm and Castle Hill cottages and the farm and buildings beyond, Brookside is still thatched.*

Landslide on Combe Martin Road, *10th January, 1919. This was reported in the Ilfracombe Chronicle on the 11th January, 1919 which stated that hundreds of tons of shale and limestone, of which the cliff and road 250 feet above Golden Cove is composed, was carried into the sea. The road also contained the gas main to Combe Martin, which was temporarily cut off. Fortunately the landslide occurred at night, and there was no damage to traffic. Golden Cove is situated on the old Coast Road beyond Watermouth Castle towards Combe Martin. One good note is that Devon County Council then built the "New Road" section from Saw-Mills up to the entrance of Sandy Cove Hotel and where the road from the village of Berrynarbor joined the coast road to Combe Martin.*

This village outing by the Berrynarbor Bellringers (c1930 Phillipse) and I am indebted to Miss Murial Richards for this copy of the photographic postcard taken by Phillipse of Ilfracombe on 4th August, 1930 above the Cliff Hydro Hotel, Ilfracombe. There appear to be 16 persons in this open charabanc with pneumatic tyres and hood! On the extreme right many will recognise "Uncle Jack Draper", who sadly died within the last few years just short of an "innings" of almost a century!

Donkeys at Watermouth. *(c1904 P). These are the donkeys as kept by Betsy Leaworthy near the centre of the village and walked daily into Ilfracombe to pick up visitors and take them for donkey rides to Lee or Watermouth etc. She is seen here standing on the right of the picture.*

"Marina Sandy Cove Hotel." *(c1930 G). This again is a seldom seen photographic postcard, by Garratt of Bristol, of the Marina allegedly named after Princess Marina who married the Duke of Kent about that time. Note the diving boards complete with ladder to ascend! Also note the slide into the pool on the left and the sets of bouyancy bags the two children in the foreground are using. At least with this swimming pool there was a complete change of water twice in every 24 hours!*

Aerial view of Sandy Cove Hotel. *(c1930 Pan-Aero Pictures). Originally built for Mr Singer of "Singer Sewing Machines" as a private residence about 1923/24. Later a Mr Rapkin bought it and opened it up as a Hotel. It is interesting to note that there is only one bungalow on Barton Lane whilst on the main road only Channel View House and Seacliffe Bungalow are to be seen.*

Watermouth Caves. *(c1930 MC). This is just one of over 60 different cards that I have depicting the caves at Watermouth, a popular spot at the turn of the century.*

Watermouth Castle. *(c1915 JS). From a water painting by A R Quinton. The Castle was completed in 1825 for Joseph Davie Bassett who also was Lord of the Manor of the lands, buildings and farms around Berrynarbor. Mrs Penn-Curzon was the last of the Bassett family to live at Watermouth but then after the Great War in 1921 the first sale of the Watermouth Estates took place including the majority of farms, cottages and land around and in the village of Berrynarbor. The remainder of the Estate (excluding the Castle and its Grounds) were offered by auction at the Manor Hall, Berrynarbor on Thursday, 5th June, 1924. Finally in September 1943, the antique and period contents of Watermouth Castle, its garages and sawmills went under the auctioneers' hammer including a Morris Cowley 12 hp car that realised £2 10s 0d, an old Russian sleigh and rubber-tyred cart £1 0s 0d and an oil painting of a man's head attributed to Rembrandt 15" by 17" realised 7 guineas (£7 7s 0d).*

During the last war Watermouth was used to accommodate army engineers and personnel connected with "Pluto" Pipeline under the ocean with a fuel line being run on the sea bed of the Bristol Channel from South Wales into Watermouth Harbour and ending at the fields below the village of Berrynarbor. It has now taken a new lease of active life with Richard and Anne Haines and family opening it to the public as a well organised show place has won several Tourist Awards and been featured on TV.

"Watermouth Castle. *(V). This early card by Valentines shows how "sylvan" a setting the castle has. On a clear day one can see the coastal beauty of the Hangman Hills and Holdstone Down as well as extensive views of the Bristol Channel and shipping as well as the Welsh coast and hills.*

Watermouth. *(c1904 P).* This is a very early card (post marked 1904) of Watermouth Harbour and shows a sailor looking out towards the open sea as well as children, probably from the village. The wooden-slatted screen in the sea, I am informed, was to protect oyster beds belonging to Squire Bassett of Watermouth Castle.

Watermouth Beach. *(p/m 1911 KB).* Smallmouth Cove with Holdstone and Hangman Hills in the background. This is another card where "Birthday Greetings" has been added making it available as a birthday card bringing back, one hopes fond memories of a holiday or visit made. The rowing boats shown here were used to ferry visitors over to Broadsands Beach eliminating a long trek and over 200 steep steps down to and, more important, up from the cove!

Watermouth Harbour. *(p/m 1904).* A different view of the harbour, postmarked 1909, shows also the main road to Ilfracombe which in common with most roads in North Devon had still only a cracked, rolled and compacted surface as can be plainly seen here.

Lee, The Fuchsia Valley. (* p/m 1904 O). *Whilst this composite card is made up of 18 views within the letters "LEE" the recipient would need a very strong magnifying glass to make out each one! On the reverse is a lyrical poem.*

The Village, Lee. (c1904 SB). *Senior and Company of Bristol published a number of very clear cards of Lee and this is no exception. Taken from just above the "Old Maids cottage", it shows the real heart of the village.*

A BIRD IN HAND.

There were three young maids of Lee,
They were fair as fair can be,
And they had lovers three times three,
For they were fair as fair can be,
These three young maids of Lee,
But these young maids they cannot find
A lover each to suit her mind;
The plain spoke lad is far too rough,
The rich young lord is not rich enough,
And one is too poor, and one too tall,
And one just an inch too short for them all.
"Others pick and choose, and why not we?
We can very well wait" said the maids of Lee!
There were three young maids of Lee,
They were fair as fair can be,
And they had lovers three times three,
For they were fair as fair can be,
These three young maids of Lee.

There are three old maids at Lee,
They are old as old can be,
And one is deaf and one cannot see,
And they all are cross as a gallows tree,
These three old maids of Lee.
Now if anyone chanced, 'tis a chance remote,
One single charm in these maids to note,
He need not a poet nor handsome be,
For one is deaf, and one cannot see;
He need not woo on his bended knee,
For they all are willing as willing can be,
He may take the one, or the two or the three,
If he'll only take them away from Lee!
There are three old maids at Lee,
They are cross as cross can be,
And there they are, and there they'll be,
To the end of the chapter, one, two, three,
These three old maids of Lee!

"A Bird In Hand!" (c1937 F).

Old Maids Cottage, Lee. (c1904 O). *This is just one of a vast number of cards depicting this famous cottage built about 1653. The "Old Post Office" can be seen in the background.*

LEE POINT AND MILL HOUSE.

Lee Point and Mill House. *(c1904 P). A very early card shows several villagers and two donkey carts – and look at the washing on the line behind the Mill house, and the large garden shelter.*

Lee Bay Hotel. *(p/m 1930). This card shows clearly how impressive the Hotel was in the 1920's; it looks as if a new bowling or croquet lawn has just been laid out in front of the hotel, and note the large garage on the corner at the foot of the hill.*

The Sea Front, Lee. *(c1908 KB). The horse and covered cart is probably the baker's from Ilfracombe and the sign on the wall reads "Manor Hotel".*

Lee Beach *(* p/m 1914 V). The large upright poles are for guiding the boats in through the rocks at mid and high tide. The message on the back to an address in Bude reads: "We shall arrive at Bude by motor Coach at 7 o'clock."*

Lee Bay. *(c1915 JS). Another postcard from J Salmon from an original water colour painting by the prolific artist A R Quinton and shows some of the coastal scenery westwards towards Bull Point Light House.*

Lee, the Village. *(c1930 Ph).* The house in the foreground is "The Hollies" which was a farm until about 1830 with lands stretching towards Chapel Cottage and the sea, and now serves as the residence of Rev Arthur Chandler who was for about 30 years rector of Ilfracombe Parish Church. The cottage next to it and half hidden by the lopped trees is the "Old Post Office" (now The Orchard) and was the carpenter's house and shop where Mr Giddey lived. Timber was cut from the surrounding woods and taken by horse and cart to the saw-mills beside the beach, and Mr Giddey made all the coffins for the Parish of Ilfracombe at only 12/6d each (62 Pence!). Again the horse and trap shown in this card is thought to be one of Mr Giddey's and he is probably driving. He also had landaus and carts.

Southcliffe Hall Hotel, Lee-on-Sea. *(c1920).* This impressive real photograph postcard of Southcliffe Hall Hotel not only gives an indication of its size but from the number of chimneys indicates that at least 12 to 14 rooms had fireplaces. The house in the foreground is "Fuchsia Glen" – as painted on the first roof.

Lee Road. *(c1908 KB). Whilst I have been unable to identify the house, the horse drawn trap was almost certainly Mr Giddey's whose grandson, John, still lives in the village.*

Lee *(c1914 PL). This unusual view taken from high up in the fields, shows part of the village but leaves the sea front hidden. The road, top centre, leads to Mortehoe and Woolacombe via Damage Barton Farm.*

The Post Office, Lee on Sea (p/m 1914 I). *Insofar as this card is post-marked 1914, it indicates that sometime after 1906 the Post Office must have been transferred to this address, just across the road from the old one.*

Old Post Office, Lee (c1904 P). *This card of the Post Office shows it was also a Tea & Refreshment House and offered the facilities of horses and carriages! Donkeys seemed to have been one of the main modes of transport at the turn of the century and one can only feel sorry for the donkey in the foreground having to take all the weight of the rotund gentleman smoking a white clay pipe.*

Ye Old Tea House, Lee. (*c1920 V). Three cards showing some of the Tea Gardens at Lee – the first shows what is now known as Smugglers Cottage on the sea front as being "Ye Olde Tea Cottage" serving teas at 9 Pence (nearly 4 New Pence) and offering "Fruit & Cream", "Ices", "Strawberries & Cream" and "Sweets & Minerals".

"The Orchard" Lee. (c1920 V).

The Orchard Tea Gardens were directly over the road from the "Old Maids' Cottage" and from the number of tables must have been very popular with parties of visitors from Ilfracombe.

"Ye Olde Farme" Tea Gardens, Lee (p/m 1906). The third card, postmarked 8th August, 1906, reads: "We have just finished a Farmhouse dinner here going to have a Paddle. Ada". Obviously a posed picture of all the staff and gardeners, with really "rustic" garden furniture, white linen tablecloths and vases of flowers. The old farm has now been converted into the "Grampus" Public House and the gardens are set out as a "Beer Garden" with tables and chairs.

Lee village. *(c1935 RA). We see here the Church of St Mathew and St Wardrede with single bell, the school room directly in front and Memorial Hall directly opposite. The circular thatched roof on the right was put there by Mr Armstrong of "Ye Olde Farm" (now the Grampus Inn) as a shelter for visitors, and part of the rounded wall is still visible.*

"Kniver Bridge", Lee *(p/m 1906). A very early card published by William Haddon of Tipton, the Footpath runs towards Bull Point Light House.*

Coombe Martin

Combe Martin Harbour. *(c1908 BG). A very interesting card, especially so because the large sailing boat in the centre is none other than the "Olive and Mary" which was originally built in Bideford and plied between all the Bristol Channel ports. The three horses and carts shown here would probably have been delivering strawberries to the boats for consignment to Wales and Bristol and there was a considerable trade of this nature. The lower slopes of the hills were devoted to market gardening with large quantities of flowers, fruit and vegetables being grown testifying to the mild climate. Beyond the rough breakwater are the "Laver-Stone" and "Camel-Rock" at the foot of Lester Point to the right.*

Harbour & Promenade, Combe Martin. *(c1908 WB). Dense woodland clothed the Combe Martin valley in those days. The Combe Martin Coat of Arms are shown in the left corner and as well as the large boats, the area on the left of the picture at the back of the "Fo'c's'le" Public House is cluttered with work shops and yards, and included a water mill which unfortunately never seems to have been photographed!*

The Fleet in the Harbour, Combe Martin. *(p/m 1909 WB). Another card in the same series. Because of the rigging, the first sailing boat is almost certainly the "Olive & Mary" and the boat with the funnel is the "Snow Flake" whose home port was Combe Martin and was used as a coal/cargo boat except in June and July when she was used for carrying Combe Martin strawberries! Snow Flake was a Clyde Puffer built in Scotland in 1893 and was bought by Captain Claude Irwin of Combe Martin a few months after his ketch sank on 28th October, 1897 off Hangman after a collision with a steam boat. Message on the back reads "Pleased to let you know I am having a ripping time at No. 12. Everything is most satisfactory & the food OK. Kind regards" and sent to Mrs Brooks at 12, Balmoral Terrace, Ilfracombe, post marked 10th July 1909.*

Combe Martin Harbour II. *(c1904 P)*. This particular view of about 1904 shows little change today apart from railings and the green shrub bushes growing outside the houses looking onto the road and harbour. The rocks and rock pools to the left have always been popular with the children. The last tall gabled building seen here was the Harbour Sub Post Office.

Seaside, Combe Martin. *(c1908 BG)*. This must have been taken sometime after the introduction of telephones to Combe Martin as there is a telegraph post beside the sea wall. Note that there were no pavements and the road surfaces were all compressed stone. The new Coast-Guard House, with white protective walls and large white flagpole is in the centre and the Harbour Sub Post Office is on the extreme right of the picture.

The Parade & Harbour, Combe Martin. *(c1930 HB). The Parade which overlooks Newberry Beach and the harbour, was built up as shown here about 1925. The white building under "Glen Avon" is the old Toll house where tolls were collected from all vehicles leaving or entering Combe Martin.*

The Harbour, Combe Martin *(c1912 PB). The sign above the large house in centre reads: "Sea Croft Boarding House Apartments". There are no railings on the sea wall and the road is lit by gas. The house on the left was the then new Coast-Guards House, now a Cafe and Gift Shop. The stream running under the bridge and beside the wall is from the river Umber which flows down the length of Combe Martin and takes its name from umber, a natural pigment similar to ochre but darker and browner, which was produced in Combe Martin up until 1882.*

Combe Martin from Berrynarbor. (p/m 1934 G). A Garratt photographic card taken from near Sandycove Hotel at around high water.

Storm, Combe Martin. (c1900). A very early photocard of what must have been a very severe storm; the crashing waves are being thrown right up and carried by the wind over the roof of "Seaview"; note the old gas lamp.

Woodlands, Combe Martin. (c1935 S). This is the entrance to Combe Martin and the seafront when travelling from Ilfracombe.

The Sea Front, Combe Martin. *(c1904). Despite the fact that this was taken about 1904, apart from general improvements, mainly to the road, there is very little change from to-day. It is interesting for those who live in Combe Martin to know that this card was sent to Miss Winnie Creek of Sheffield House, Combe Martin. This part is known locally as the "Strand", and the railings were in front of "Sea Croft".*

A "bit of Combe Martin" *(p/m 1905 M). Also addressed to Miss Winnie Creek in 1905. Combe Martin church can just be seen on the right behind the thatched roof. The cottages in the centre are Engine Tenements and the building in the far background is Park House.*

A bit of Combemartin.

Combe Martin High Street. *(p/m 1908 M). "Delve's Temperance Hotel" is on the right and what a pretty terrace of thatched cottages. This card is postmarked "Combe Martin R.S.O. Devon 1908" and the message: "We are here for the day, it is a sweet little seaside place."*

Old Combe Martin. *(p/m 1908 Stills Series). Thatched cottages by Pound Lane, which leads to the village pound where any stray sheep or cattle would be tethered up pending being claimed by their rightful owners. The "Comers" lived in the thatched cottage on the left, and Combe Martin church can be seen just behind the tree.*

A Devonshire Lane, Combe Martin. *(c1910 PB). To reach this lane turn left halfway down the village, opposite the road to the Church and Barnstaple, up Corner Lane which leads to Knapp Down and the old Silver Mines. This steep narrow lane exemplified various types of the real old Devon lanes cut out of solid rock and through high banks of earth before meandering across open ground.*

St Peter's Church, Pewter Flagon, & Silver Gilt Chalice & Paten. *(1634). Published by Twiss Brothers of Ilfracombe about 1906, on its reverse is printed "Old Altar Vessels", Combe Martin Church. "Inside the Chest is kept a curious set of Pewter Altar Vessels, and some old keys inscribed:- The guift of Thos: Ivatt of Combemartin, Esquire. July 1 Anno Dom 1634"*

Crackie Lane, Woodlands, Combe Martin. *(c1912 F). Another picture of rural tranquility with a local lad on the footbridge crossing the small stream that finds its way down to the sea via Newberry Beach.*

Combe Martin, Parish Church and Reuben Dale "The Mighty Atom". *The church is believed to have been founded by Martin de Tours or his son, Robert, soon after 1088. It is interesting to note that in 1827 the four church bells were recast into six bells, then in 1922 these six were taken down and recast into eight bells and mounted on a new metal frame. Three years later in 1925 the church tower's four large pinnacles were rebuilt. The tower is very impressive having four stages and being 99 feet to the top of the battlements, and is similar to the towers of Hartland and Berrynarbor, and on one map postcard of North Devon is written:*
"Hartland for length, Berrynarbor for strength: Combe Martin for Beauty."
Inside the church is a very impressive wooden screen.
Reuben Dale was known as "The Mighty Atom" from his many boxing fights, largely staged in Cornwall.

Combe Martin from Park Hills. *(p/m 1921 P). One of several view cards of the village produced and published by The Pictorial Stationery Co Ltd, of London under the "Peacock Autochrom" label. This one shows the central area with the church as the centre piece.*

Combe Martin from Barnstaple Road. *(c1908 P). A very interesting "Peacock" card, it shows in the foreground the limestone workings known as "Berry's Quarry" which were worked from about 1840 until 1916. The limestone was mined and then transported on tramways – the lines are just visible on the card, those on the left running to the "spoil" or waste heaps, and one to the right ending at the limekiln visible to the left of the cottage/farm house on the right. Coal (culm) would be shipped from South Wales to Combe Martin harbour where it would be unloaded onto horse and carts and taken to the many limekilns in the village. In the limekilns layers of local-mined limestone would be covered with layers of the Welsh "Culm" and then set alight and roasted to slake the lime which was then collected by the local farmers to "sweeten" their acid soils and increase yields. The card also shows clearly just how long the High Street is with houses either side of it.*

Woolacombe & Mortehoe

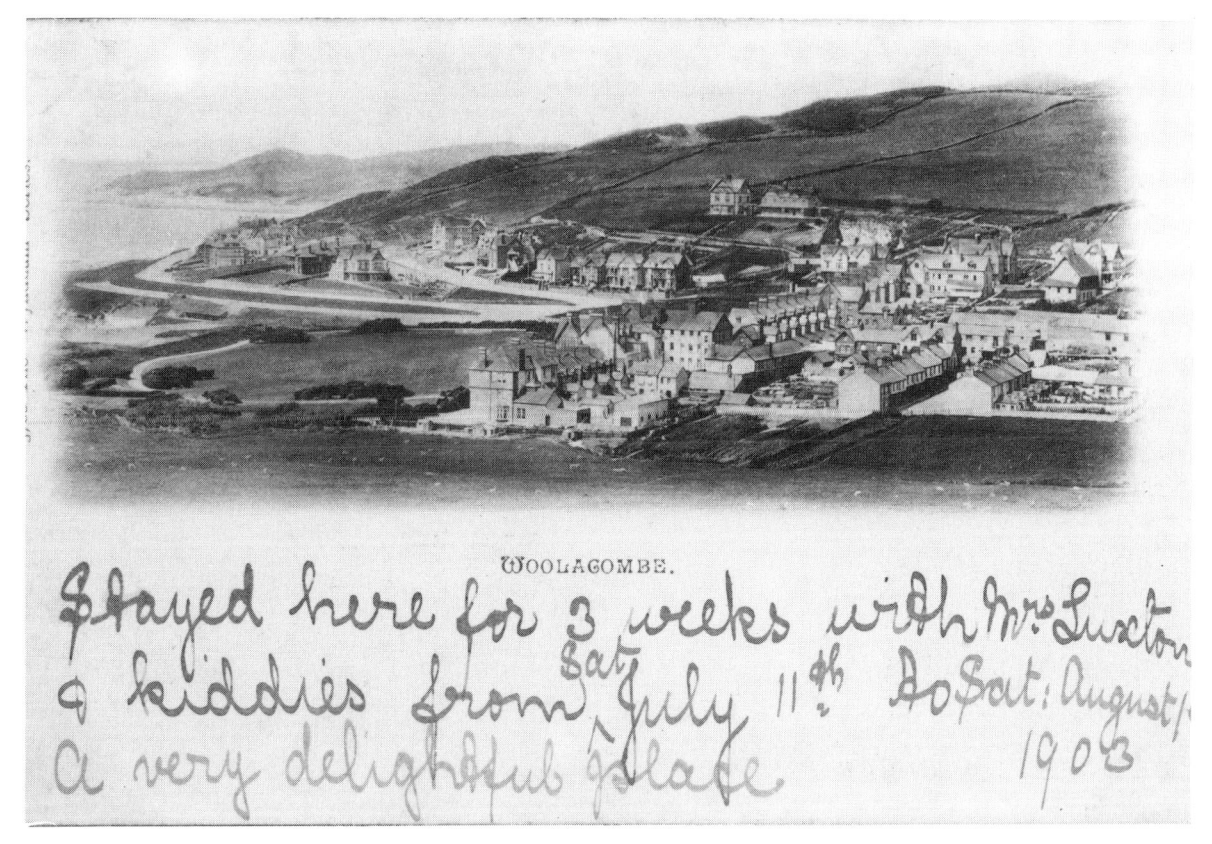

Woolacombe. *(c1903 Wy) Woolacombe as it was about 1902.*

Rounders on Woolacombe Sands. *(p/m 1909 P). Full of action; canvas deck chairs remain virtually unchanged to date, but the front and hillside are now much more built up. The large house on left with columns, Parade House but now called White Breakers, was built for Rosalie Chichester who had become the sole heir of Arlington Court and Estates when her father, Sir Bruce Chichester, died in 1881. The large double fronted house to the right was built for her Land Agent and is now called Hartland House.*

Woolacombe Sands. *(p/m 1906 T). Punch & Judy Shows were very much expected on the beaches at that period and we see here a number of children and adults looking at a performance in progress. The large cliff of spoil and tippings at the top of the beach were from the excavations for Simpson's Garages in Barton Road, and now called Barton Court.*

Woolacombe. *(p/m 1905 P). This picture of the Beach, produced about 1904 under the "Peacock Autochrom" label, was published by Charles Clark, The Library, Woolacombe. In those days white bell tents were hired out to the many visitors in the same manner as the wooden chalets are today. But what a difference then with hardly any "flesh" to be seen at all and one lady holding up an umbrella to ensure the suns rays didn't reach her delicate, white powdered face!*

The Sands, Woolacombe. *(c1919 V).* *This card by Valentines was commissioned by F Beer of Woolacombe and as well as the cliffs leading out to Baggy Point, shows the then new beach huts, as well as the white canvas tents of different appearances and sizes.*

Donkey riding on Woolacombe Sands. *(c1906 IC).* *This charming card shows how the Victorian/Edwardian young lady was expected to ride side-saddle, even on donkeys. Note the large covered shelter overlooking the beach, and the top of then Southcombes Restaurant, now known as the Red Barn.*

Coombes Gate & Watersmeet. *(PG). Watersmeet Hotel can be seen in the foreground whilst the others are, from left to right: Crows Nest, Craigside, Sunnycliff, Point House, Blue Bay, Gull Rock, Haven Hotel and Combeside.*

Barricane Shell Beach, Woolacombe. *(c1911 F). Large bell tents were used by Parkers in providing Teas and Refreshments about 1911 when this photographic post card by Friths was taken. Morte Point can be seen at the end of the peninsular on the right. Barricane is said to be an anagram of Carribean where many of the tropical shells that are washed up on to the beach are said to have come from, brought over by the Gulf Stream.*

Barricane Shell Beach, Woolacombe. *(*c1911 F). Another card by Friths, taken at the same time as the one above, but looking landwards. The large house on the left is Barricane Hotel, next is the Beach Hotel, and finally The Castle which was built about 1897.*

Woolacombe Bay Hotel. *(p/m 1919 V). An early card of the Bay Hotel posted in 1919 when the hotel was boasting: "Situated in its own extensive Pleasure Grounds of about six acres. Sloping down to the far-famed Woolacombe Sands. Contains spacious Dining Hall, Lounge, Drawing, Smoking, Writing, and Billiard Rooms; Children's Dining Hall and Children's Playroom; Cycle Room, & c. Fine Sea and Coast Views, including Lundy Island, Morte and Hartland Points. A Perfect Health Resort. Thorough Comfort. Experienced Chef. Gas throughout. 200 Apartments. Reduced Tariff October to March. Motor Garage. Telephone No. 7. Golf Links (18-Hole, very sporting course) two minutes from Hotel."*

Woolacombe from the Golf Links *(*p/m 1909). As well as Woolacombe Bay, this view shows Granville Terrace, The Bay Hotel and, just behind, Rosalie Terrace (after Miss Chichester), Bank Terrace and Station Road with, up on the right, the original wooden church that was pulled down about 1912.*

The Cafe and Granville Terrace, Woolacombe. *(c1919 PG). This fine card is one of many published by P. Goss, 2 The Crescent, Mortehoe and shows a truly uncommercialised Woolacombe, even Southcombes Restaurant blends into this setting of tranquility. The large house to the right and up from the gas lamp is where the Narracott Grand Hotel now stands!*

Mortehoe, Sands and Bay. *(c1920 Ph)*. From Morte there is a breathtaking-view of Woolacombe Sands, Baggy Point, Hartland Point, Morte Point and Lundy Island. The building in the foreground is the Mission Hall.

Clay Park, Mortehoe. Taken prior to the last war, a single-decker bus from Ilfracombe is in the area reserved for turning, note the two old cars and amount of housing.

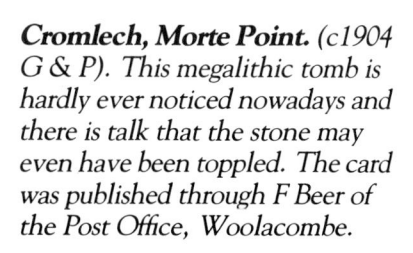

Cromlech, Morte Point. *(c1904 G & P)*. This megalithic tomb is hardly ever noticed nowadays and there is talk that the stone may even have been toppled. The card was published through F Beer of the Post Office, Woolacombe.

The Old Bells of Mortehoe. *(1926). A real gem of photographic postcards, showing the vicar of Mortehoe Church, the Rev T Daffen, and Church Warden Mr G Smalldon (on left) with the Mortehoe Bell Ringers; Messrs:- A Smith, E Norman, T Watts, W Hill and A Brown (left to right) behind the complete set of six bells, removed for recasting in 1926. Behind the church lych gate the Mortehoe Post Office can just be seen.*

Mortehoe Church and Lych Gate. *(c1904 P). The perpendicular-styled church dates back to before 1200 and has a very impressive lych gate and just to the left can be seen, showing between the gravestones, the chimney pots of the "Chichester Arms" Public House.*

The Look Out, Mortehoe. *(c1920 Ph).* The covered Look Out Station, used by coastguards for many years, has a clear view of the Bristol Channel from Hartland right round to Bull Point and taking in Lundy Island. The Look Out Station was built in 1914 and was completely removed in 1982! A tablet can be seen just to the left of the door.

Putsborough Sands, also known as Vention. *(p/m 1938 K).* Putsborough Sands Hotel has replaced the long, low building, with laid-out gardens in front of the road. The very large buildings up on the hillside were those of Heathercombe Hotel which was sadly burnt right down during the last war, with the death of the cook. The house next to the beach is Vention House and clearly visible is the old lime kiln.

Putsborough Manor. *(c1935 K).* This large Manor House still looks very attractive but can no longer boast a thatched roof.

South View from Hunters Inn. *(p/m 1909 M).* The buildings just beyond the cottage on the left now provide refreshments and gifts for the many visitors, particularly coach parties, that come here in summer. One can only surmise that the occupants of the two horse-drawn coaches are partaking of liquid refreshment in the Hunters Inn whilst the horses have been let loose in a field.

Hunters Inn and Valley. *(c1908 T).* Apart from the loss of its original thatched roof, the idyllic Hunters Inn has changed very little.

The Beach, Heddon's Mouth. *(c1908 M).* Heddon's Mouth has always been a place of great natural beauty and no visitor should miss it despite the mile walk from Hunters Inn, the closest a car can get to this remote spot. A large limekiln impressively stands at the top of the beach and has recently been renovated.

Woodabay! (p/m 1904 T). *This early picture shows the ill-fated pier built so that coal (culm) and limestone could be brought direct by boat from South Wales for use in the limekiln that can be seen near the beach to the left of the pier. It was hoped that passengers would be landed by the then many paddle steamers bringing visitors for all the Bristol Channel ports. Unfortunately within only a few years the pier had been reduced to rubble by the frequent storms and was never rebuilt; some of the remains can still be seen today.*

Martinhoe. (c1908 M). *James Hannington, who was the martyred first Bishop of Eastern Equatorial Africa was associated with both Martinhoe and nearby Trentishoe.*

The Post Office, Woody Bay. *(p/m 1908 M). This appears to be not only a Post Office but also a Private Hotel as on the back the writer says "This is where we are staying and we visited Lynton yesterday".*

Glen Hotel, Woody Bay. *(c1908 M). The Glen Hotel is now known as The Woody Bay Hotel and has always been a popular hotel for visitors and for honeymooners. The views across the Bristol Channel to Wales are fantastic, particularly at sunset when the pinkish hues add to the spendour.*

Lee Abbey

About 1570 the family of "Wichehalses" escaped the persecution of the Protestants instituted by Philip II of Spain by fleeing with their fortunes to the secure and beautiful retreat of Lee Bay, on the shores of North Devon. The Wichehalses settled, built, married and flourished and in the reign of Charles I. Jennifried de Wichehalse, the young and beautiful heiress of the house, was betrothed to a nobleman in high favour with the Court. Sadly on the wedding morning a messenger brought tidings that her faithless lover had deserted her and was now married to another. So distraught was she that in the evening she wandered from her home and when next day dawned, her lifeless body was found at the base of precipitous cliffs which formed the rugged promontory of Duty Point – now called locally "Jennifer's Leap". However, there was a fitting retribution in store for on July 5th, 1643, the Parliamentary forces, under Sir William Waller, encountered the Royalists at Lansdown, near Bath. De Wichehalse had joined the ranks of the people, and Lord Auberly, the betrayer of his daughter, was in high command on the King's side. During the first charge of battle the two met and crossed swords in deadly combat and eventually Jennifried was avenged by the death of her destroyer, Lord Auberly. Sir Bevil Grenville of Bideford was also killed in the same battle! Unfortunately the King's troops invaded the quiet valleys of Lynton a year later and the Wichehalse's were all lost when they tried to escape by putting out to sea in rough weather from Lee Bay – and in sight of the ill fated Duty Point! The land and Lee Farm and "Six Acres" then passed to John Short until 1735 when they were assigned to William Knight and then in 1784 were assigned to John Clarke. Then in 1841 by a deed of sale passed from the Clarke family to Mr Charles Bailey who became Squire of the Manor and restored the Entrance Arch and Tower and about 1850 built the main house as a gentleman's residence and pretentiously changed the name from Lee Farm to Lee Abbey. Upon Charles Bailey's death it passed into the ownership of his son, Mr CF Bailey. After the First World War the house was in danger of becoming derelict and was bought by a Company who turned it into a Hotel in the 'twenties' with Tuck's producing several real photographic postcards of it. Sadly, with the depression of the 'thirties', the venture failed. During the Second World War the Abbey was given a new lease of life when it was transformed into a temporary home for an evacuated Preparatory School.

Directly after the War the Right Reverend Dr Cuthbert Bardsley, Bishop of Coventry, with a group of friends, set up a charity Trust called the Lee Abbey Fellowship and they purchased the property together with 360 acres of land for £28,000. The purpose of Lee Abbey being to provide a centre which guests could visit for holidays, conferences, study courses and so on and has grown steadily up to the present time with many hundreds of Christians from all over the world coming annually to participate in the fellowship offered there. Lee Abbey won a "Heritage, National Landscaping Award" in 1976 and claims to be the largest self financing mixed religious community in Europe.

Miss Denbridge's Tea Gardens, Lee Bay, Lynton. *(c1935 V). Whilst this cottage is now part of the large Lee Abbey Estate Fellowship, scrumptious "Devon Cream Teas" are still served there in summer and offer excellent value and the opportunity to take the short walk down to picturesque Lee Bay.*

Lee Abbey. *(c1904 P). The Abbey has grown over the last 50/60 years. This photo was taken about 1904/06. Many later cards show it as Lee Abbey Hotel and state; "Original entrance to Old Manor House. Sundial over Porch dated 1650, the Gate-Tower entrance originally built in the days of Charles I was restored in 1830.*

Lee Bay and Abbey. *(c1928 JS). From another water colour painting by AR Quinton showing the old derelict tower on the hilltop as well as Lee Abbey, its estates and Lee Bay. As with many bays on the North Devon Coast this had its own limekiln.*

93

Lynton

Lynton. The Castle Rock.

The Castle Rock, Lynton. *(c1902 P). The Castle Rock stands majestic here with the headlands of Lee Bay and Woody Bay in the distance. A beautiful view published by the Pictorial Stationery Co., Ltd. under the "Peacock" label, before 1903 as it has space on the reverse side for only the address with any message being written on the white space beside the picture.*

Valley of Rocks, Lynton. *(*c1910 M). An early photographic postcard by Montague Cooper who had offices in Lynton, Taunton, Wellington, Bridgwater, Burnham and Chard. It is interesting to note that an entrance between two stone pillars in the foreground of the picture has been infilled with similar dry stone wall construction as that surrounding the entire field, and is where cricket has been played now for nearly a century!*

VALLEY OF ROCKS. LYNTON.

Lynton. Town Hall.

Town Hall, Lynton. *(c1908 PPC). Given by Sir George Newnes to celebrate his son's 21st birthday and costing upwards of £15,000, this fine building displays to the best advantage the fine Old English style of architecture. In appreciation the residents of the twin villages commissioned a handsome bust of Sir George which was unveiled in the entrance hall of the Town Hall by Sir Arthur Conan Doyle. The assembly hall is upstairs where dances and theatre performances etc. are held. On the skyline is Sir George's impressive residence, Hollerday House and the gate posts to the right form the entrance to the driveway.*

Lynton. *(c1911 F). This card shows Valley Road extending to Lee Road, the Town Hall and forecourt, with the Wesleyan Chapel next to it whilst opposite we have the shops. Long dresses and parasols protect from the sun's rays.*

95

Prideauxs Car Hire Depot, Lee Road, Lynton. (*c1928 M). From the advertising signs on this highly collectable card one must presume that the three different model cars are all "Austins". The car in the centre, has more modern spoked wheels, and the headlamps on the first car look like huge search lights. Note, too, the opportunity of hiring an "open" or "closed" car complete with chauffeur, and the 'phone number of "21".

Heather Farm, Lynton. (c1908). Where the fire in the old hearth was said to have been kept burning for over 300 years, and that was around 1908! The farm is situated at Cheriton on the small lane up towards Hoaroak from the Hillsford Bridge over Farley Water. Farmer Will Squire lived there in the '30's whilst Richard Squire lived at Manor Farm on the other side of the lane.

Convent of Poor Clares, Lynton.
The Refectory.

Convent of Poor Clares, Lynton. *(c1930 M). This is one of several cards produced and shows the Refectory. With religious troubles in France in 1903 a group of five Poor Clare nuns from Rennes came to Woodchester in England and were, in 1904, through the kindness of Father Hugh Lean, given a villa in Lynmouth to set up as a temporary Convent. The Foundation Stone for the Roman Catholic Convent and Church was laid on 23rd October, 1908 and the building was completed in 1910 with the Poor Clares entering their new convent on 18th March, 1910 with the first mass being held the very next day, the Feast Day of St Joseph. The land and the cost of building the entire Church and half the Convent was given by Father Hugh Vincent Lean as a thanksgiving for the gift of faith. The community of approximately 20 consists of enclosed Sisters, and Extern Sisters who are engaged in the external duties of the Convent. (For much of the above information my thanks to Sister Bernadette who was most helpful and has been at the Convent since 1940! and I believe must have been one of the many British girls to seek admission to the Order.)*

In the Stocks, Lynton Church Yard. *(*c1903 P). What a picture, taken by "Palmer" about 1903 and published by "Peacock", it beautifully displays the hob nailed and "horseshoed" boots which at that time were worn by both parents and children.*

Lynton, St. Mary's Church, South Entrance. *(c1906 JW Strangward, Lynton)* The church was largely rebuilt in 1741 and was considerably enlarged in 1904. The Church registers date from 1591 and there is a monument recording the demise of Hugh Wichelhalse of Ley in 1653. There is a peal of six bells in the tower. Just beyond the church can be seen the Valley of Rocks Hotel which was famed for its impressive central lounge where cast iron columns rose through three floors and supported a coloured glass ceiling.

LYNTON, Church, South Entrance.

Lee Road, Lynton. *(*c1906 W)*. **The Congregational Church** on the left was one of many gifts given to the twin villages by Sir George Newnes, costing about £1,500 and originally dedicated on 23rd August, 1904. Further along Lee Road at the junction with Park Street is the Lynton branch of W H Smith & Son, who were "Booksellers, Librarians and Newsagents". Further up the road is Bellvue Avenue and Crossmead whilst the houses of Park Gardens can be seen through the gap between church and shop. Strange how in this photo we have pedestrians walking in the road and the farmer on horseback is on the wrong side of the road.

Lynton Church and Castle Hill. (*c1929 F*). This photo by F Frith was taken in 1929 and is full of interest showing the wonderful cars and charabancs crowding the square. The first charabanc is advertising a trip to Doone Valley and Hunters Inn. Trips to Porlock, Watersmeet, Woody Bay, Valley of Rocks, Lee, Ilfracombe, Combe Martin, and Barnstaple were also made. The column on the left is part of the Valley of Rocks Hotel.

Castle Cottage Hotel, Lynton. *(c1907 F). A very early card of this hotel, with the lovely thatched ground floor extensions and quaint Victorian chimney pots.*

Lynton. *(*c1904 M). A real photographic postcard by Montague Cooper taken about 1904 or earlier, as Cross Street and Queen Street are the only roads crossing from the main road (Lee and Valley Road) over to Lydiatt Lane. Sir George Newnes (The London publisher and great benefactor to Lynton & Lynmouth), lived in Hollerday House, a great mansion, which he had had built about 1893/4 just below the summit of Hollerday Hill (800 ft). Unfortunately just after it was sold to Sir Thomas Hewitt in 1913 it was completely burnt down. The Royal Castle, the Imperial, The Valley of Rocks and the Lynton Cottage Hotels are all visible, whilst the small school can be seen in the foreground.*

Lynton from Hollerday Hill. *(c1911 F). This card by Friths was taken in 1911 and shows the recently completed Roman Catholic Chapel and Convent of Poor Clares in the left foreground. The two cross roads are Bellvue Avenue and Crossmead which run into Lydiatt Lane and Park Gardens. The new road to Barnstaple was later built across the field at the back of the terraced houses and is now used to enter Lynton from that direction. Park Farm can be seen on the 'Old Barnstaple Road' (Lydiatt Lane) top centre and the large house to its right is Rock Lodge. The large house in the foreground is Sandrock, to the right of which can be seen two of the three Long Mead terraces.*

Lynton from S.W. *(* F) This could be a photographic card by Francis Frith, in which case it was taken about 1893. It is taken from the Old Barnstaple Road (Lydiatt Lane) with Park Farm on right, the thatched haystack and farm building nearly opposite having disappeared in the first quarter of this century! On the left can be seen Lee Road with the Town Hall and Cross Street opposite. Park Gardens Terrace is in line with the square church tower, with Countisbury and Foreland Point in the distance. The pointed towers either side of the church are Valley of Rocks Hotel and Imperial Hotel.*

The Cliff Railway, Lynton. (* M). *On Easter Monday in 1890 Sir George Newnes, who was also the benefactor, performed the opening ceremony of this, the first such railway, based upon two platforms, each capable of carrying 20 passengers, connected by an endless cable passing round large pulley wheels at the top and bottom of a double set of rails running sheer down a cliff face with a gradient of 1 in 1¾ for 900 feet, thus rising/falling 450 feet. The system remains unchanged; each platform has a very large tank underneath which is filled with water at the top and emptied out sufficiently, at the bottom so that the top platform becomes heavier and pulls up the lower; each platform has automatic and emergency brakes. This scheme had been worked out by Bob Jones, a local engineer, about 1870 and only became a reality with the financial backing of Sir George, who is the gentleman on the left of the platform in this picture. In 1916/17, and before Lynton Hill was tarmacced, cars were transported up or down on the cliff railway by moving the carriages off the platforms and it was said "This is now the general practice as the damage done to the tyres in negotiating the steep Lynton Hill entails greater cost than the car fare by Cliff Railway." The fares were: Up 3d, down 2d, return 4d; Motor Cars, 7/6d for small cars, 10/6d for large cars.*

Directions Hill, Lynton. *(c1911 F).* This shows just how steep, how slippery and how stony Directions (Lynton) Hill really was. Surely the majority of passengers would want to get out at the top and walk down, particularly when thinking how high up pasengers sat and how the carriages could sway and rock!

North Cliff House, Lynton. *(c1911F). Not only Northcliff House, but also second stopping point for the Cliff Railway with a small platform from which to enter the carriage. The sign on the wall is a notice from the Cliff Railway Company. Whilst the stopping point has not been regularly used for probably half a century or more one can still see the original wrought-iron gates access from either side of the railway.*

Lynmouth

Lynmouth. (p/m 1914 JEJ). This composite view card by Jay Em Jay shows eight views, comprising four of Watersmeet and the Lyn Valley with the remaining four depicting Mars Hill, Rising Sun Inn, The Harbour and Rhenish Tower, and finally the Lyn Bridge River.

Mars Hill, Lynmouth. (*p/m 1912 I). A card full of character, with the local horse and cart and well-dressed visitors with their boater hat's and parasol. Look particularly at the four just going up Mars Hill past the Rising Sun which is advertising "Mild and Bitter Ales, Drawn from the Wood, by S W Arnold & Sons of Taunton". The small shop is selling postcards, cream teas etc. The tall white building on the left is Manor Cottage and was used as the "Pixie Tea Rooms". Just beyond can be seen the Lifeboat House which had a Territorial Institute upstairs and was, unfortunately a victim of the flood disaster. It was replaced with a Memorial Hall with an exhibition on the first floor commemorating that dreadful night of 15th August 1952, when disaster struck this quaint old fishing village.

The Rhenish Tower which was built by a General Rawdon about 1800 as an exact replica of a tower on the German River Rhine. It was used as a beacon light for entering Lynmouth Harbour and was a flood disaster victim.

Lynmouth, "Waiting for the Steamer". (*c1907 F). A much clearer view of the paddle steamer, with passengers waiting to board the rowing boats back to the steamer.

Lynmouth Harbour. (c1920 F). This shows four heavily loaded passenger rowing boats making their way back to the paddle steamer anchored in the bay and waiting to return them to Minehead (13 miles), Weston Super Mare (50 miles), Wales (36 miles) or Ilfracombe (13 miles) after their visit to the twin villages.

Lynton & Lynmouth (c1908 T). This photographic post card by Twiss Brothers of Ilfracombe shows most of the main buildings in the twin towns including the ill-fated Hollerday House seen on the hilltop. The large house halfway up the hillside on the left is Maysmore House now divided into two. Clooneavin Footpath linking the foot of Lynmouth Hill with Lynton lies directly behind Maysmore. Note, too, the boats anchored up beside the Rhenish Tower and the Esplanade hugging the cliffs on the right. The cutting aiming directly up towards Sir George Newnes home is the cliff railway.

The Coach, Countisbury Hill, Lynmouth. *(c1904 F). Most of the occupants were expected to get out and walk up the hill behind the coach as it climbed Countisbury on its way to Minehead. On this occasion there was also an army officer walking up with his bicycle! Six horses were needed for both the climb and descent of the hill, hence the man and two horses infront. Message on reverse – We are becoming mountaineers, you never saw such hills to climb as these are here.*

Minehead Coach, Royal Castle Hotel & Grounds! *This card below, produced by Friths both to advertise and for use by the "Royal Castle Hotel", is included to show how many cards were "doctored/ adapted" by the publisher. I leave it to you to note the many differences, all false!*

Coaching at Lynmouth. *(p/m 1928 G L Gunn, Lynton). Here the fully-laden coach is seen making its way out from Lynmouth on the very beautiful and ever meandering road which runs along the valley of the East Lyn towards Watersmeet. A policeman stands in the middle of the road between the Lyndale Hotel and the Granville House Hotel.*

Lyndale Hotel & Minehad Coach. *(*c1908 D). This "Lynton Minehead Stagecoach" complete with the six horses for climbing Countisbury are seen here waiting for remaining travellers before setting off on the three hour journey to Minehead. As photographic post card by E T W Dennis & Sons Ltd.*

Lynmouth Hill *(c1911 F). The stage coach approaching the last steep bend. The two leading horses would probably only be used to the top of the hill and then wait to assist other stages with the steep hills of Countisbury and Lynmouth.*

107

Beach House and Quay, Lynmouth. *(c1910 M). This somewhat unusual view shows the Quay; Beach House is in the centre with a flat roof and parapet and later became Beach Hotel and was a flood disaster victim. The posters on the wall make interesting reading advertising "J R Davis's Drug Stores for all types of Medicines" and South Western routes to London via Lynton and Ilfracombe, also to the Midland Counties and the North.*

The Glen Lyn, Lynmouth. *(c1907 F). Below is another view that has completely changed since the flood disaster of 1952. Note the almost church-like windows of the building on the right.*

Old Lynmouth (c1908 PPC). Now a historic card as unfortunately with the flood disaster in 1952 the building on the left known as "Sunnyside" disappeared and where the river then flowed has now become the roadway. It is interesting to see halfway along how one householder has apparently tried to build out over the river – was it used for illegal fishing of salmon or trout?

Mars Hill, Lynmouth. (c1915 JS). A water colour by AR Quinton and published by Salmons, shows how artistic licence allows lamp and telephone posts and any other ugly "modern" inventions to completely disappear overnight!

Mars Hill, Lynmouth. (c1915 JS). Mars Hill in the opposite direction again by "ARQ", as AR Quinton is more popularly known amongst card collectors.

LYNMOUTH. — Lyn Bridge and Lyndale Hotel. — LL.

Lyn Bridge and Lyndale Hotel *(c1930 LL)*. In common with all "LL" cards, which were printed in France, the detail and clarity is exceptionally sharp. Note the open touring car with spare tyre – imagine changing a tyre instead of a wheel – the "AA" sign on the corner of the hotel and the electric lamp protruding out from the flagpole.

Lynmouth from above the Bridge. *(c1930 S)*. The hotel on the corner is the Granville Private Hotel and parked on the road just beside the River Lyn is a large open car and an open charabanc. One of the small shops is Elworthy, Grocer and the East Lyn Cafe and finally Bevan's Lyn Valley Hotel.

Lyndale Bridge, Lynmouth. *(c1933 F)*. At the bottom a line of cars arriving at Lyndale Bridge after descending Countisbury Hill: they have to decide whether to go straight on for Lynton and chance the 1 in 4 gradient of Lynton Hill, turn right for Lynmouth sea front, or left for Lynton, Ilfracombe and Barnstaple via Watersmeet.

The Lynmouth Flood Disaster. *August 1952, Lynton Hill Corner. (c1952 F). This shows very clearly the terrific force of the floods, as here at the foot of Lynton Hill the road and bridge were completely destroyed. The colossal rocks and boulders were in some cases brought miles down the river and were so large that they had to be reduced to a manageable size by drilling and filling with dynamite. The explosions were carried out on a daily basis for months! Altogether thirty one persons lost their lives in this terrible and natural disaster which had worldwide press coverage. However, this wasn't the first flooding to occur in Lynmouth as in 1607 the stormy sea swept many houses away including an entire row of cottages near the shore, forming one side of the field on which the Manor House now stands. Then in 1910, a great tidal wave completely covered the esplanade and the lower part of Lynmouth, doing enormous damage to walls and roadways.*

Lynrock Mineral Water Spring and Bottling Company. *(c1920 M). This was built on the East Lyn just downstream from Myrtleberry where there has always been a natural spring of pure and crystal fresh water. "Lyn Rock" water was said to possess valuable medicinal properties. Sadly the entire buildings and bridge were carried away in the 1952 Flood Disaster. Although the bridge and path have been replaced the only reminder of these premises is the ever-flowing spring and the opportunity to take a cool refreshing natural drink. A part of one of the original marked bottles can be seen beside the commemorative plaque.*

Woodside, East Lyn, Lynmouth. *(c1920 V). This romantic looking building helps to perpetuate some of the reasons why Lynton and Lynmouth are often referred to as the "English Switzerland". It is all the more sad when one realises that this was another casualty of the floods and is no longer there. A Valentine card, published by J G Richards, Tobacconist of Lynmouth.*

Glen Boarding House at the foot of Lynmouth Hill. Glen Boarding House In common with the majority of other Lynmouth hotels, has fancy carved weather boards to the gabled ends of the slated roofs. This card was published by Slann's Creamery, Granville House, Lynmouth.

The Head of the Glen, Glen Lyn, Lynmouth. (c1915 Myrtleberry Series). Just one of many spectacular sights to be seen in Glen Lyn. Others include the Long Falls, the Horseshoe, Seven Falls, Rustic Bridge, the Top Fall, and the Steps. They used to belong to a Mr K W Riddell and the entrance Lodge Gates for the grounds were opposite Lyndale Bridge and were open to visitors on Tuesdays, Wednesdays and Fridays when a small fee, generally expected, was put in a box and distributed to the poor at Christmas.

Lynmouth Church *(c1904 P). St. John's Church. The large house on the left is Aberlyn House and that on the right is Heather Villa. The Foundation Stone was laid on the 24th June 1869 by Bishop Trower and opened for worship in August 1871. The church was later enlarged by the addition of an aisle about 1915 to the memory of Mrs. Adkins, formerly Miss Lock-Roe of the Manor House.*

Old Bridge near Lynmouth. *(c1903 P). This bridge over the East Lyn River swept away in the floods could hardly have been made from more natural materials, even the majority of the central supporting pier is a huge boulder, whilst whole tree trunks support a series of cut and cross laid timbers covered in gravel and stone. The man is rod fishing, probably for salmon or trout, whilst the three visitors on the bridge are undoubtedly posing for this photograph.*

Myrtleberry, East Lyn. *Upstream from the Lyn Rock spring and downstream from Watersmeet on the East Lyn River. About 1916 it was known as the Myrtleberry Refreshment House and was approached by a light and graceful bridge under which was a miniature water-wheel, barely two feet across, but sufficient to supply motive power to drive machinery for domestic purposes. This early card shows the orderly vegetable gardens, the lawns with deck chairs and tables follow the curve of the East Lyn, and the footpath can be seen on the far side.*

Watersmeet and Cottage, Lynmouth. *"A Happy Christmas to You". (˙c1911 F). This treasured card shows how cards were used as greetings by a simple yet effective overprint. There are so many different views of this famous beauty spot that they could form an entire collection and this is just one of over one hundred and fifty! Watersmeet Cottage has been providing cream teas for nearly a century and now belongs to the National Trust. Visitors can watch the many birds, including dippers and nuthatches, whilst enjoying their lunch or tea, or can browse around the National Trust Shop within Watersmeet Cottage.*

Dean Steep. Lynton Hill. Countisbury Hill. Beggars Roost. Porlock Hill.

FAMOUS WEST COUNTRY HILLS

116